Big Head!

DR. PETE ROWAN

For my daughter Grace

www.randomhouse.com/kids/

First American edition, 1998

Library of Congress Cataloging-in-Publication Data

Rowan, Peter.
Big head! / Peter Rowan ; illustrations by John Temperton.
p.   cm.
Includes index.
Summary: Examines the various features of the body associated with the
head, particularly the brain and how it functions.
ISBN 0-679-89018-1
1. Brain — Juvenile literature. 2. Head — Juvenile literature.
[1. Brain. 2. Head.] I. Temperton, John, ill. II. Title.
QP376.R76   1998
612.8'2   dc21   97-39009

Printed in Singapore by Tien Wah Press (Pte) Ltd.

1 3 5 7 9 10 8 6 4 2

Design and Art Direction by Peter Bennett
Consultant for anatomical illustrations: Lydia Umney

Acknowledgments
The author would like to thank his friend Dr. John Pilling for his help in checking the facts in this book.
Special thanks — as usual — to Kate Petty, for being a wonderful editor.

Big Head!

DR. PETE ROWAN

ILLUSTRATED BY
JOHN TEMPERTON

ALFRED A. KNOPF
NEW YORK

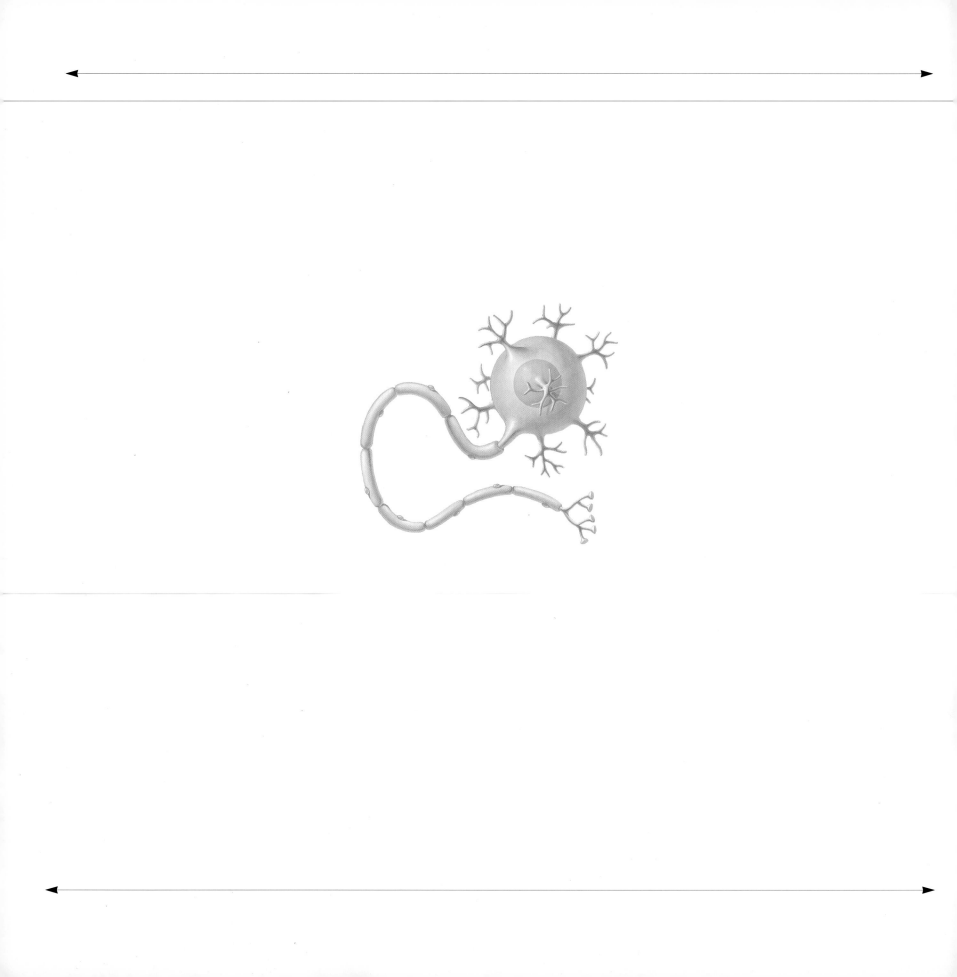

Contents

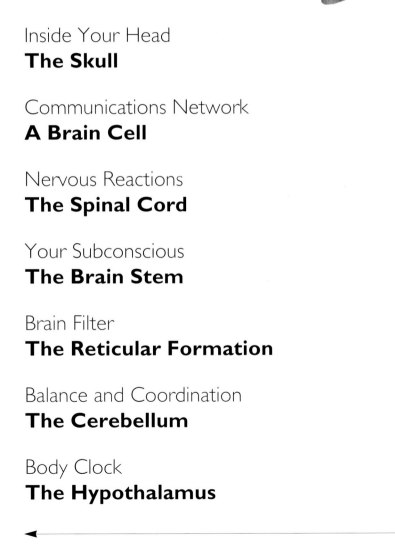

Introduction

A re you a Big Head? The answer is Yes! Human beings have large heads compared to total body size. And in particular, it is the upper portion of the brain – the cerebral cortex – that is the largest part of the head. What this means is that you have on your shoulders now one of the most amazing creations ever seen by the eye – itself an incredible part of your Big Head. Turn the pages of this book and you'll see all the stages of construction as a whole head and its brain are assembled. Along the way, discover some of the things that this most complex living tissue on Earth can do for you: from speaking your mind and expressing your personality to more practical matters such as eating, protecting your brain, and feeding and watering your body.

And the exciting thing about the brain is that the more you use it, the better it gets at the tasks you give it. Use your head with the tests and experiments in this book and you'll certainly improve your Intelligence Quotient (IQ).

T he most brainless animal that ever lived was *Stegosaurus* ("plated lizard"), which roamed the United States 150 million years ago with a brain the size of a walnut. This tiny brain controlled a body that weighed almost 2 tons and measured 30 feet long!

FACE FACTS

Y our brain was assembled in a way similar to the brain in this book. Over eight months before you were born, a simple, tiny tube of tissue began to develop inside your mother. This would become your brain and spinal cord. The tube became bent in some places and swollen in others, until your amazingly complex nervous system took its final shape.

USE YOUR HEAD

Could you weigh your head if you wanted to? I weighed one once when I was an anatomy student at medical school. It had been cut off its body and had belonged to a man. I put it in a bag and hung it on a scale. It weighed about 6.5 pounds. There are three ways you could weigh your own head. The most accurate method would be to cut it off (keeping the blood) and put it on a scale. This isn't really practical and can be exceptionally messy.

The next method would be to lie on the floor and put it on a bathroom scale. This wouldn't be very accurate because your neck muscles could not completely relax, holding up your head and making it seem lighter than it really is.

The third method uses a bucket of water. Fill it to the brim, then stick your head in. The water will overflow. Take your head out and then fill the bucket up again, carefully measuring the water needed to reach the brim. This equals the amount of water your head displaced. One quart (32 fluid ounces) of water is roughly equal to two pounds (32 ounces), so if your head displaces one and a half quarts of water, it weighs 3 pounds. This method assumes that your head and water are the same density. They are not exactly, but the heavier bone is offset by the lighter air-filled cavities of your sinuses, and as your brain is 85% water anyway, it is fairly accurate.

The human with the smallest known adult brain was Daniel Lyon. He lived in New York about a hundred years ago. He could read and write and he worked as a night watchman for 20 years before he died. His brain was half the weight of yours and only 6 ounces more than an ape's. Amazingly, he lived a normal life. This probably means that people like you and me, with normal-sized brains, can achieve much more with them than we actually do. In other words, the potential of your brain is enormous!

FACE FACTS

A new way of taking pictures (PET scans – or Positron Emission Tomography) of a living brain enables us to see the brain in action. For the first time it is possible to produce images of your brain as you think and do things – like reading this book and speaking about it later to your friends. You can literally see pictures of your brain making up your mind.

The largest brain on Earth is the 20-pound brain of the sperm whale. However, that is only 0.02% of the whale's weight. The human brain weighs in at about 3 pounds, but this is 2% of our body weight. So how big is yours? Does size matter? If you're a girl, it's probable that your brain is slightly smaller than the brains of the boys in your class. This may be an interesting fact, but it doesn't mean much – brain size is not linked to intelligence.

Look at Yourself

The mind: the most elusive part of the human body

Hold the opposite page up behind your head and look into a mirror for a moment.

In this book you will find images of how your head and your brain would look if you could actually see under the skin. Right now you can look in the mirror and see yourself as the world sees you. And you are looking at a living example of one of the most complex creatures ever to have roamed the Earth.

As you look into your eyes, you see much more than just a face. You are looking into, and thinking about, your mind. Abstract ideas like mind, personality, will, spirit, and intellect are impossible to picture, but they make up what many people consider to be the very soul of an individual: that which, to quote the dictionary, is "the spirit or immaterial part of a person, the part of you that survives after death."

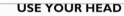

USE YOUR HEAD

What sort of personality are you? Would you describe this cup as half full or half empty? Optimists are supposed to say half full and pessimists half empty.

Boys vs. girls

Modern PET scans of the brain show a very few subtle differences between boys' and girls' brains. How such differences come about, and what their effects might be, are a mystery. In any case, what counts is not your gender, but the use that you as an individual make of your enormous brain power.

Einstein's brain

After the renowned physicist Albert Einstein died in 1955, his brain was removed and preserved in a bottle. People thought that if they studied his brain, they could find out why his mind was so brilliant. Of course, the powers of his mind – its electricity and chemistry – had long since gone when the brain turned up in 1978, pickled in formaldehyde under a beer cooler in a doctor's office in Kansas.

Beauty box

What is a beautiful face? Computers have been used to try and measure loveliness mathematically. Key distances, such as eyes to nose, nose to mouth, and mouth to chin, have been fed into a computer and compared. Startling similarities were discovered between many famous beauties. However, one face in particular did not fit the computer's blueprint – Marilyn Monroe's eyes were too far apart and her nose was too short! Many saw this exception as a victory of chemistry over computing.

FACE FACTS

The Greeks thought the soul was situated somewhere around the pituitary gland (see p. 27).

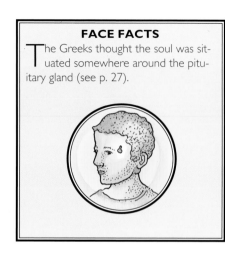

The Mind and Personality

Watch this space. It will help you to locate what you are looking at in the main picture.

The **eyes** — windows of the soul?

Eyebrows — can they indicate how intelligent you are?

Is your **mouth** smiley, sensuous, grim?

Do the **proportions of your face** conform to the ideals of beauty?

Does your **chin** give away your attitude?

Highway to the Head
The neck: fastest speedway in the body

Your neck is the superhighway to and from your head. While you are at rest, air is being sucked down into your lungs at about 6 mph. (Give a cough and it might shoot out at 100 mph!) The next time you take a drink, the fluid will travel down your esophagus (gullet) at speeds approaching 0.4 mph. Right now blood is rushing along your arteries at nearly 2 mph (though it is returning to your heart in veins at a more leisurely pace). But as you read this, the fastest speeds occurring anywhere in your body are along your spinal cord in your neck, where messages to and from your brain are hurtling along spinal nerves at roughly 270 mph.

Your airways, esophagus, blood vessels, and nerves are the visible roadways for traffic inside your neck. There is also a less obvious but just as crucial transport system: the endocrine system, which is controlled by chemical messengers called hormones. The thyroid gland is a good example of one of the body's endocrine glands. The ultimate control is from your brain's pituitary gland (see p. 27), but under its guidance your thyroid gland sends hormones into your bloodstream to affect the growth, waste disposal, and energy of nearly every cell in your body.

Along the superhighway of your neck, traffic moves continuously, day and night, between your body and your head.

USE YOUR HEAD

To locate some of the most vital structures of your neck, lie on a bed and lift up your head. The sternomastoid muscles can easily be felt as a strap down each side of your neck. Underneath them lie the carotid artery, the internal jugular vein, and the vagus nerve. This nerve comes from the medulla (part of the brain stem) and runs through your neck to your chest and abdomen. Its branches transmit messages to your heart, lungs, intestines, and other organs. Through the vagus nerve your medulla controls your heart rate, blood pressure, breathing, and digestion without your having to have any conscious control over these complex functions. Next time your stomach rumbles, that's your vagus nerve at work.

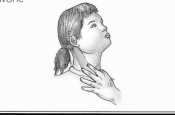

All neck

Giraffes grow taller than a double-decker bus. Half of this height is neck. A giraffe has to have an incredibly strong heart to pump blood up to its head. There are also valves in the neck's blood vessels to prevent the rush of blood to the head that might otherwise happen when the giraffe bends down! Like you, the giraffe has seven neck bones (cervical vertebrae) – they each just happen to be 11 inches long!

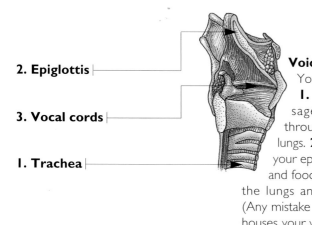

2. Epiglottis

3. Vocal cords

1. Trachea

Voice box

Your larynx has three jobs: **1.** It is part of the open passageway, your trachea, through which air enters your lungs. **2.** It contains a "trapdoor," your epiglottis, that helps direct air and food in the right direction – to the lungs and stomach, respectively. (Any mistake here and you choke.) **3.** It houses your vocal cords – two bands of tissue that can make noises (your voice) as air passes between them.

The Neck

Your neck is probably about the same length as my son Edward's (see top right), but the longest neck ever measured was $15\frac{1}{2}$ inches! It belonged to a woman of the Padaung tribe in Burma. Traditional Padaung women stretch their necks by fitting copper rings one on top of the other to form a column.

The **carotid arteries** supply oxygenated blood to your head.

The **jugular veins** drain blood away from the head and neck and back to the heart.

The **thyroid gland** sits like a butterfly over the trachea and secretes hormones that regulate growth and metabolism.

The **trachea** carries air to and from the lungs during breathing.

Spinal cord

The word **esophagus** (gullet) comes from two Greek words meaning "to carry to eat," which is exactly what it does – from the mouth to the stomach.

Vagus nerve en route to the rest of your body. It helps regulate your heart rate, breathing, blood pressure, and digestion.

Larynx – the origin of the sound of your voice (behind thyroid cartilage).

Inside Your Head

The human head: the most complex living tissue anywhere on Earth.

Imagine that you could peel back your face. Suddenly the unique appearance on display to the rest of the world is gone, because unless you have an identical twin there is no one else in the world with a face like yours.

First remove the skin and the hair, as if the face were a mask. This would be a very bloody business because of all the arteries, veins, muscles, and nerves that wind over your face.

Sitting underneath all this tissue is the bony case of the skull. Safe within its protective case and watching the world through your two eyes is the brain itself. Here, beneath a spooky collection of 22 bones, is the essential you.

As you read on, you will trace the single basic unit of your brain – the neuron or brain cell – through all the parts that build up into the incredible structure that sits proudly on top of your shoulders: your **Big Head!**

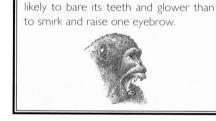

FACE FACTS

Girls' faces are on average 20% smaller than boys'.

The plump cheeks on a baby's face enable it to suckle more efficiently and comfortably.

Humans rely on the face to relay subtle meanings far more than other primates do. A chimp is more likely to bare its teeth and glower than to smirk and raise one eyebrow.

Hair
Humans have much less hair than most of the other 4,000 varieties of mammals. Nowhere is this more obvious than on the face, although many men shave off most of their facial hair every day. One theory about the differences between the sexes is that they make recognition easier at a distance. A beard, for example, indicates a man – someone you might wish to meet with, or someone to avoid if he looks fierce.

Evolution of the face
Humans have flat faces, with eyes at the front and a short nose. We can see the same object with both eyes, giving us keen binocular vision, but our sense of smell is relatively weak. Compare this with the primitive head of the shark, which has eyes on the sides of a very long nose with a terrific sense of smell.

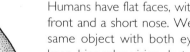

Brain surgery
Surgeons usually get to the brain by drilling a hole in the skull over the area on which they wish to operate. We know from prehistoric skulls that this approach, called trepanning, has been around for thousands of years! Other ways in are through the nose or along the blood vessels in the neck.

The Skull

The skull is the most complex bony structure in your body. Most of its 22 bones are flat. All the bones, apart from the lower jaw, are linked tightly together by zigzag joints called sutures. The lower jaw is attached by hinged joints.

The cranium

or braincase has evolved over millions of years into a rounded structure that allows for the maximum amount of brain within the minimum amount of skull.

The eye sockets

are deep and safe containers to protect your eyes.

The 14 facial bones

provide a frame for the muscles that move your face. These bones also protect the delicate sense organs of smell and hearing.

Teeth

guard the mouth – the hole through which they cut up and chew the food that will become you. You really *are* what you eat!

SKULL AND CROSSBONES

In many cultures the skull is a powerful symbol of death. Pirates used it on their flag, the Jolly Roger (probably from the French *jolie rouge*, "pretty red" or "bloody"), to strike terror into the hearts of their victims.

The lower jaw

is the only mobile bone in the skull. Your clenched jaws are so powerful that your bite can lift an object as heavy as your own body.

Communications Network

Brain cells: the cells in your body with the longest life

Inside your Big Head right now there are about 100,000,000,000 living nerve cells (also known as brain cells or neurons). Each one has hundreds of connections with other nerve cells, and electrical impulses are buzzing around their circuits like balls in a super-charged pinball machine. This maze of nerve fibers will control every body cell as you work your way through *Big Head!* As you move, think, remember, sense, and feel, they are at work. Being special cells, they have special features. They can't store energy, and they need a continuous supply of both food (glucose) and oxygen. So you must be eating and breathing to get through the book safely. Unfortunately, if nerve cells die, they can't be replaced – they are lost forever.

FACE FACTS

Nerve cells carry electrical messages in one direction only – sensory messages to the brain and motor messages out of it.
Individual nerve fibers tend to be grouped together into visible "nerves."
All your "thinking" is done by electricity and chemicals!

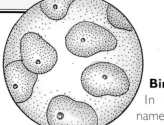

Bird brain cells

In 1872 an Italian scientist named Camillo Golgi accidentally knocked a piece of owl's brain into a solution of silver nitrate. After several days Golgi took it out and looked at it under his microscope. He saw cells that had been stained by the silver nitrate. These were the brain's neurons. Golgi was the first person ever to see a single neuron. He won the Nobel Prize for his cell studies.

Simple minds

The hydra is a jellyfish-like creature that spends its life attached to weeds or rocks in freshwater ponds. Life is pretty dull in a pond, and a hydra's days are a fairly simple business. It doesn't move much and does little more than use its tentacles to catch food that happens to drift by. Instead of a brain it has a simple nerve network. If something interesting happens in the pond, then an electrical message slowly spreads around this network. Humans' lives are more lively and complex than a hydra's, so we have developed a collection of neurons that we call the brain and spinal cord.

USE YOUR HEAD

You can measure how fast nerve impulses travel through your head. Ask someone to drop a ruler between your thumb and forefinger. You must react quickly without knowing when it will be released. Measure in inches how much of the ruler has fallen before you catch it.
This is the sequence of events. You see the ruler move and visual messages travel along the optic nerve into your brain. The brain reacts and sends a message to your hand. Both electrical transmission (along nerves) and slower chemical transmission (at synapses) are in action here, and the whole process may be over in 0.2 second. The fastest nerve cells are carrying messages along their axons at an amazing 130 yards per second (268 mph).

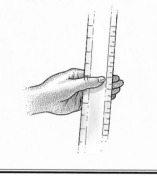

A Brain Cell

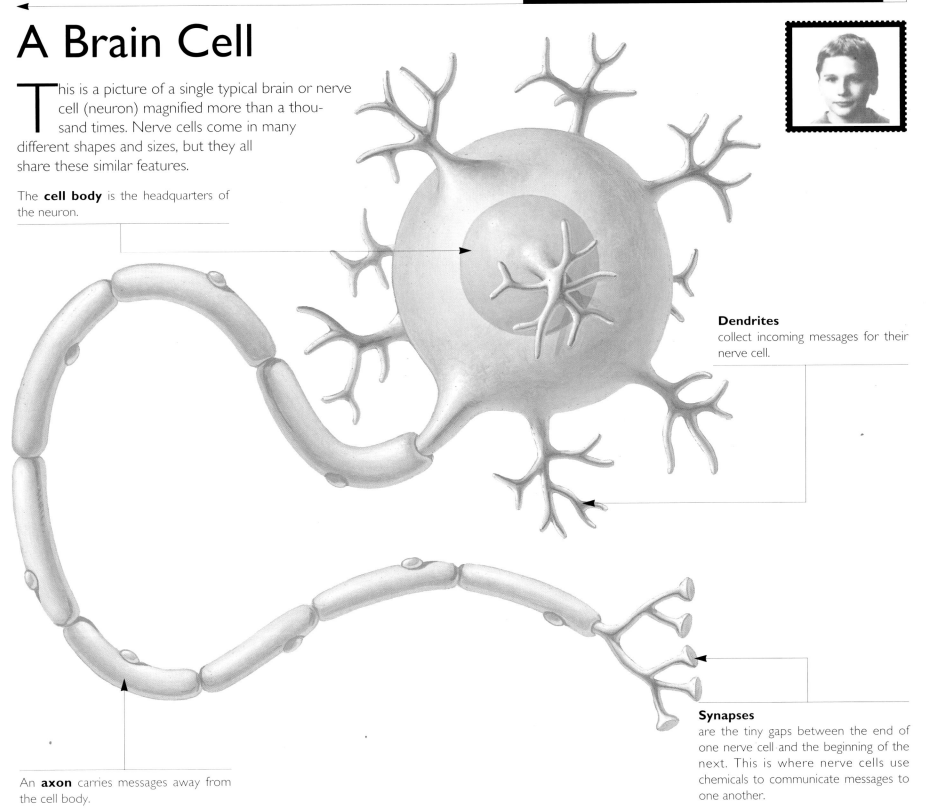

This is a picture of a single typical brain or nerve cell (neuron) magnified more than a thousand times. Nerve cells come in many different shapes and sizes, but they all share these similar features.

The **cell body** is the headquarters of the neuron.

Dendrites collect incoming messages for their nerve cell.

An **axon** carries messages away from the cell body.

Synapses are the tiny gaps between the end of one nerve cell and the beginning of the next. This is where nerve cells use chemicals to communicate messages to one another.

Nervous Reactions

The fastest type of nervous reaction

is the reflex

There are about a million motor nerves coming down the front of your spinal cord from your brain's cortex (see p. 30) at this very moment. These nerves control hand actions, like turning pages, and leg movements, like crossing your legs. They are carrying impulses as you sit reading this book. Meanwhile, information from your senses is entering the back of your spinal cord to travel up it and be appreciated by your brain. Information such as pain, touch, and temperature (hot or cold) arrives from nerve endings in your skin. And important messages about the position of your body come from special sensors in your muscles, joints, and tendons.

Inside your head there is a system of four connected hollows: caves and tunnels shaped something like a prehistoric bird in flight. They are called ventricles. Sloshing around in these caverns right now is a pale, watery liquid called cerebrospinal fluid (CSF). About half a cupful of this fluid flows around the outside of your brain within membranes called meninges (see p. 33) and your brain floats in it. This arrangement supports the soft, jelly-like brain, which would otherwise collapse under its own weight. Cerebrospinal fluid is filtered from the blood by knots of capillaries that hang from the roofs of all four ventricles.

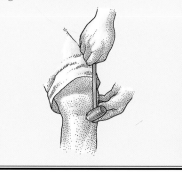

(DON'T) USE YOUR HEAD

It's easy to show a spinal cord reflex in action. Cross one leg over the other at the knee and ask a friend to tap your knee just below the kneecap. When the correct spot is hit, your knee will jerk up. Impulses have gone from the knee to the spinal cord and then immediately back down to the leg muscles that straighten the knee.

Brain bypass

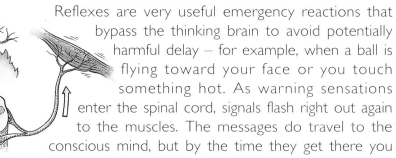

Reflexes are very useful emergency reactions that bypass the thinking brain to avoid potentially harmful delay – for example, when a ball is flying toward your face or you touch something hot. As warning sensations enter the spinal cord, signals flash right out again to the muscles. The messages do travel to the conscious mind, but by the time they get there you have ducked out of the way or taken your hand off the hot plate.

Renaissance discovery

Leonardo da Vinci was one of the first people to realize the real shape of the ventricles inside the brain. For thousands of years before, they had always been drawn as spheres. Leonardo poured hot wax into the ventricles of a dead ox to reveal the true shape of the system shown in blue on the opposite page.

FACE FACTS

Nerve speeds may be the swiftest phenomena in the natural world, but they are slow compared to some modern inventions. If you were a giant, 35 miles tall, and you stood on a sharp thumbtack just as a rocket was launched by your foot, the message about the tack would reach your ankle just as the rocket whizzed past your head.

The Spinal Cord, Ventricles, and Cerebrospinal Fluid

The spinal cord leaves your skull through a large hole and runs down as far as your lower back within your backbone. It's about 15 inches long. The "gray matter" in the center is mostly nerve cells. The "white matter" outside the cells consists of bundles of nerve fibers going to and from your brain.

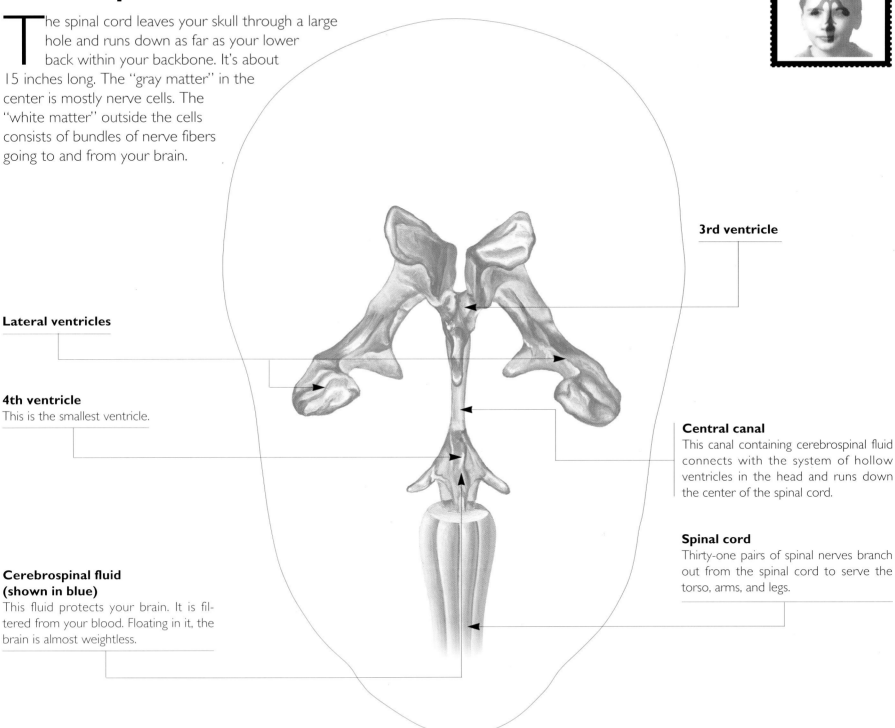

3rd ventricle

Lateral ventricles

4th ventricle
This is the smallest ventricle.

Central canal
This canal containing cerebrospinal fluid connects with the system of hollow ventricles in the head and runs down the center of the spinal cord.

Spinal cord
Thirty-one pairs of spinal nerves branch out from the spinal cord to serve the torso, arms, and legs.

Cerebrospinal fluid (shown in blue)
This fluid protects your brain. It is filtered from your blood. Floating in it, the brain is almost weightless.

Your Subconscious

The brain stem: the only part of the the nervous system without which life is impossible

As you read this, just 10% of your brain tissue stands between you and sudden death. The brain stem is the only part of the nervous system to have this power. What makes it even more remarkable is that most of the time you're not conscious of what it is doing.

Here in the brain stem lie the rigidly programmed clusters of nerve cells necessary for survival. While you are reading this book, they are subconsciously controlling your heart rate, blood pressure, and breathing, as well as the transport of your last meal through your intestines. From here, signals can flash out like thunderbolts to spark off coughing, sneezing, hiccuping, or vomiting.

THE IMPORTANCE OF DREAMS

Dreams are obviously important. In an experiment carried out several years ago, a cat deprived of the dreaming phase of sleep died after 20 days. One theory suggests that we use dreams as a time for discarding unnecessary information rather than storing it in the long-term memory. This theory has the unlikely support of the hedgehog-like echidna, which has a huge brain for its size. This egg-laying marsupial does not have REM sleep (so perhaps does not dream) and may need its large brain to store all the information it doesn't dream away.

Dream on

Last night and again tonight, and probably every night for the rest of your life, a small cluster of 30,000 blue cells in the part of the brain stem called the pons will begin to fire. This is where your dreams are born. During the dreaming phase of sleep, your cortex builds up these impulses from the pons into a kaleidoscope of the adventures that we call a dream. This seems to be a time when your brain sorts out or tidies up various memories, thoughts, and experiences.

Scientists can monitor dreaming because dreams occur mainly during the rapid eye movement (REM) phase of sleep, and these movements under the closed eyelids are easily visible.

INTERPRETING DREAMS

The Austrian psychoanalyst Sigmund Freud said that dreams were the "royal road to the unconscious" and wrote a book about interpreting them. He believed a dream in which you are pulled from water symbolizes birth – as in leaving the fluid in which all babies float before birth. Here are some other common interpretations of dreams:

Falling: worry about failure at school or in exams.

Being naked: feeling over-sensitive or vulnerable.

Flying: confidence.

Reptile brain

In reptiles and fish, the brain stem forms the main part of the brain. The cerebral cortex, which is the seat of emotions and conscious thought, is tiny and poorly developed. So don't expect to be greeted with a smile from the tortoise or a wag of the tail from the goldfish when you come home from school.

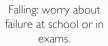

The Brain Stem

The brain stem connects the spinal cord to the rest of the brain. The three parts of the brain stem – the pons, the midbrain, and the medulla – are each about an inch long.

The **midbrain** coordinates head and eye movements. It contains the highest number of motor neurons in the central nervous system.

The **pyramids** are huge bundles of fibers that make a landmark on the medulla. They carry messages for skilled controlled movement from the cerebral cortex to the body's muscles.

The **pons** is mainly made up of tracts of nerve fibers linking the cerebral cortex with the cerebellum (see p. 25), and the spinal cord. The pons controls sleep and dreams.

The **medulla** controls heart rate, breathing, and blood pressure. It also contains the brain's vomiting center.

Brain Filter

The reticular formation: the supreme gatekeeper to your conscious mind

Interesting as this book is, if an elephant suddenly charged toward you now, I bet you would very quickly notice it. As the ground rumbled, the room vibrated with trumpeting sounds, and two large tusks flashed by your throat, you would become aware that the largest living land animal was breathing down your neck. But the arrival of the elephant would be only a fraction of about 100 million pieces of information being fed into your nervous system at that moment. Information from your eyes, ears, tongue, nose, and the touch receptors in your skin would still be arriving at the gateway of your nervous system. What's taking your mind off all of these inputs and allowing you to notice the elephant?

The answer is that 99% of all the information coming to you is filtered out by a piece of brain stem not much bigger than your little finger. Your reticular formation (RF) is continually sorting and sifting incoming messages and allows only what might be necessary or important — maybe the sudden smell of smoke — to be "appreciated" by the higher parts of your brain. Without the RF you would literally go crazy.

The reticular formation
The RF enables the tennis player to concentrate only on hitting the ball — shutting out all the distracting information coming into the brain. Players often find they go through a big game without hearing the shouts of the crowd or feeling the pain of an injury until the match is over.

FACE FACTS
The RF can also register the absence of sensations the brain has become accustomed to. People living by a railroad get used to the noise of trains running while they are asleep, but can be woken up if a familiar train fails to run past their house!

Homework in front of the TV
The RF is kept active by all its incoming information and in turn it keeps your cerebral cortex "awake." Parents are often baffled when their children insist that they can work with the TV on. But the children might be right! It is possible that the increased work for the RF in filtering out all the extra distractions keeps the cerebral cortex alert.

USE YOUR HEAD
Take off your watch. Feel the watch and then put it on again. Your skin will register all the sensations as you do this. Maybe the watch is cold or feels rough or smooth. Then put your arm behind your back. After a few moments your RF begins to filter out the messages from the skin around the watch and it becomes quite difficult to tell if you have a watch on or not!

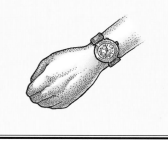

The Reticular Formation

This is an intricate connection of nerve cells extending through the core of the brain stem.

The exceptional feature of the **reticular formation** is the large number of connections it makes with other parts of the brain and spinal cord. The 10 dark brown clusters shown in the picture are clusters of RF nerve cells. Impulses from these nerve cells literally keep the rest of the brain awake, making the RF the arousal center of the nervous system.

Drugs

The effects of drugs on the brain are clearly seen in spiders and the webs they weave.

1. Unfinished web of a laid-back spider on marijuana.

2. Drunk spider falls asleep on the job.

3. Shaky web of an anxious spider on a high dose of caffeine (coffee).

"MIND-EXPANDING" DRUGS

The drug LSD (lysergic acid diethylamide) reduces the action of the RF. Users may suddenly find increased awareness of sensual perceptions that might otherwise have been filtered out, such as sounds and colors.
LSD has very curious effects on animals. Siamese fighting fish float nose up, goats do silly walks, and spiders spin fantastic but useless webs. One elephant dropped dead after being given LSD. It's best avoided, as it is potentially a very dangerous drug.

Balance and Coordination

The cerebellum: the part of the brain with the most nerve cell connections

S top reading these words for a moment and bend your head back to look up. Then ask yourself this question, "Do I know where my feet are?" You do, of course, even though you can't see them, just as, if you decided to take a few steps, you wouldn't have to look down and check their position. The reason you can do these actions without thinking about them – and much more complicated things, like riding a bike or running down stairs – is because of a computer-like part of your brain called the cerebellum ("little brain"), which functions like the autopilot of a plane. It's continually receiving information about the position of your body from your eyes, ears, and the nerve endings near your muscles and joints. It processes all this so that your body can move around in a smooth and well-balanced way without your thinking brain – the cerebral cortex – being involved.

Try "thinking" about running down stairs . . . It's much easier to let the cerebellum work out the movements on its own for this!

Cat walk
A cat has a large cerebellum for its size. This is partly what is responsible for its typically graceful movements and usually enables it to land on its feet no matter how it falls.

Evolution
Australopithecus boisei, an ancestor of modern humans who lived almost two million years ago, had a large, well-developed cerebellum. The space for it can be seen in fossil skulls. Stone axes and other tools found with the skulls show that this early hominid had finely coordinated hand movements. The chimpanzee, our nearest primate relative, has a smaller cerebellum and less precise hand movements, but it uses simple tools, such as straws or sticks for poking things and stones for cracking nuts.

Heavy metal
The first visible signs of a cerebellum that isn't working properly are what you would expect – a reeling, staggering walk, slurred speech, and shaky hands. The metal mercury can damage the nervous system, and in particular it targets the cerebellum. In many countries mercury is used to dress seed before it is sown to protect it from fungi as the crop grows. There was a large-scale epidemic of cerebellar disease in Iraq a few years ago when bread was made from mercury-dressed seed rather than from the crop that the seed should have produced.

The Cerebellum

The cerebellum makes up about 11% of your brain. Folds in its surface keep 85% of it hidden from view. In cross section it looks like a small cauliflower (see p. 41).

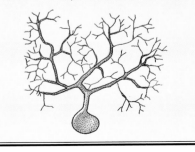

THE MOST COMPLEX BRAIN CELLS

PURKINJE CELLS

The nerve cells of the cerebellum – Purkinje cells – are among the most complex brain cells you have. They are tree-shaped and the "branches," or dendrites, may make contact through synapses with 100,000 other nerve fibers – more connections than any others in the brain.

Cerebellum

Like the rest of the brain, the cerebellum has a left side and a right side. If you feel your head at the back, around where the hairline ends, these two "computers" are just under the surface.

Body Clock

The hypothalamus: the most accurate clock in your body

T icking away inside your head right now is your biological clock – a living timepiece controlled by your hypothalamus. It follows roughly the solar 24-hour cycle of day and night and takes its cues from the light levels coming from your eyes. Very few parts of your body escape its influence. This "clock" is a group of cells within the hypothalamus no bigger than a few grains of sand!

It's 10 a.m. as I write these words. By this time of day, most of us are completely awake and brain activity is at its peak. Unless your biological clock has been upset – perhaps by jet lag – you can check your watch or a clock and see where you are in today's time cycle (right).

12 noon Appetite is stimulated for food (energy).

10 a.m. Fully alert. Kidneys on full power and forming urine.

2 p.m. Many people feel slightly sleepy after lunch. This could be the effect of digesting the food.

8-10 p.m. Depending on your age, your body is ready to "clock off" and rest for 8-10 hours.

6 p.m. Dusk falls (the exact time depends on the time of year). A hormone is secreted that tends to cause sleepiness.

3 a.m. Body temperature falls. Heart slows. Urine production falls. Episodes of REM sleep and dreams occur. Brain activity is reduced.

8 a.m. Heart rate and blood pressure go up as you begin to move around. Draw the curtains and the light of the rising sun confirms with your brain's clock that it really is time to begin an active day.

6 a.m. Body temperature rises. Chemicals prepare the body for activity. Energy stores are mobilized.

The Hypothalamus, Thalamus, and Pituitary Gland

The hypothalamus is located just under the egg-shaped thalamus and at 0.14 ounce (the size of four peas) makes up 0.5% of total brain weight. However, for its size it has no rivals in its great influence over your body's activities. The pituitary gland helps control your endocrine glands, which in turn control your hormones. The thalamus works with the "thinking" brain (the cerebral cortex) to organize information from your senses.

Thalamus
The thalamus has only a basic appreciation of sensations, such as whether something is pleasant or unpleasant. It is here that receptors interact with drugs to relieve pain.

Pituitary gland
Hormones secreted by this gland include growth hormone. People who are extra tall or extra short may have some problem with their pituitary gland.

Pineal gland
This is sometimes called a "third eye" because, although it is deep inside your brain, it receives information about light levels from your eyes and is involved in setting your body's clock.

Hypothalamus
This regulates your autonomic nervous system. It influences many different body activities such as blood pressure, heart rate, breathing, body temperature, appetites for food, drink, and sex, as well as movement of food in the gut. It is also the center for your emotional responses (see p. 29), making you ready to run when you are scared, for example.

Emotions

The limbic system: the most emotional area of your body

The limbic system is the mysterious bubbling cauldron in which all your pleasures, pains, and memories are brewed – your "emotional brain." At the moment it is impossible for me to tell what's going on in that part of your brain, because events in the limbic system depend on personal things, like your past life, your memories, and what has influenced you.

Most of the time your limbic system balances your emotions. However, sometimes the limbic system may be almost overwhelmed by emotion and, if its electrical activity spills over to the brain areas that deal with movement and language, you may become paralyzed by fear or left speechless. Because the limbic system is so closely linked with areas that deal with heart rate and digestion, like the hypothalamus, it's not surprising that emotion can also play havoc with these functions in the form of high blood pressure and stomach ulcers. The ultimate blow the limbic system can deliver to its own body is death. Terrible grief and emotion can even cause the heart to stop.

Your emotional brain stores at least two sorts of memory. **Fact memory** holds names, dates, facts, and faces. These can be very easy to forget! Once in the long-term memory, they are usually filed along with an experience. So if you meet friends while swimming on vacation, you'll remember them in the pool in their swimsuits. **Skill memory** holds activities such as riding a bike. Unlike facts, these are very difficult to forget. Skills like tying your shoelaces are almost impossible to "unlearn."

USE YOUR HEAD
(Don't try this!)

A Spaniard named José Delgado implanted an electrode into the limbic system of an aggressive bull. He then stood in front of the animal with his transmitter. The bull charged as soon as it saw him, but when Delgado fired the transmitter, the bull stopped immediately and became very friendly!

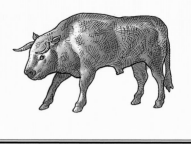

FACE FACTS

Déjà vu means "already seen" in French, and it's that feeling of something having happened before. Maybe you visit a place you've never been to and feel you've been there before. *Déjà vu* may occur because for some reason your brain has stored your first impressions as if they were recalled memory.

Nostalgia

Because memory is handled in the limbic system, it's no surprise to discover links between memory and emotions. And because the sensation of smell enters the brain through the limbic system, smell is the most emotive of all the senses. It has the power to trigger powerful memories. I have only to return to my old school and smell the floor polish to remember exactly what it was like to take exams, be yelled at, and look forward to summer vacation. There will be odors that do the same for you!

Short-term and long-term memory

Short-term memory (STM) lasts about 30 seconds – just about long enough to dial a phone number before you forget it. Use a particular STM often and it will be converted to long-term memory (LTM). LTM must involve permanent changes in the brain, as many memories last a lifetime. Repeating facts as well as understanding them improves the transfer of STM to LTM.

The Limbic System

The limbic system is a wishbone-shaped arrangement of nerve tissue wrapped around the top of your brain stem. It links the lower parts of the brain with the higher reasoning centers of the cerebral cortex. Your sense of smell – unlike your senses of sight, taste, hearing, or touch – is plugged directly into it.

The **fornix** is a bundle of fibers carrying messages of memory and emotion from the hippocampus.

The **mammillary bodies** are two pea-like structures that relay smell impulses.

The **hippocampus** is essential for learning. It converts short-term memory into long-term memory.

The **amygdala** is where fear learned from experience is stored. A rat with its amygdala removed has been known to lose all fear of cats!

Thinking, Learning, and Speaking

The cerebral cortex: the most human part of the brain

It is from your cerebral cortex that you think, see, hear, imagine, but most humanly of all, that you speak your mind! (And maybe later decide to change it, too.) Please quietly read the next sentence out loud. You are now using the most brilliant technical achievement of the brain. (You can stop now.) What you just did sets you apart from all the other animals on Earth. Imagine where TV, radio, books, schoolwork, and conversation with friends would be without language. All of us remember and think in words.

Now you can try out your thinking brain. **1.** Look around at any object close by you. **2.** Now say the name out loud. **3.** Your brain is hearing the word as you say it. **4.** Finally, the most interesting part of the experiment: think up something to say about the object. For example, if your object is a pencil, you might think, "That's something I can write with."

Speaking sentences is a much more complicated event than the simple outline above. Your teacher suddenly asks you a question in class. You must choose the correct words, organize the grammar, and then physically speak the words – all in a split second.

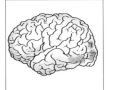 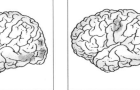 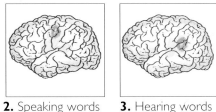 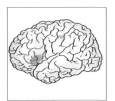

1. Seeing words   **2.** Speaking words   **3.** Hearing words   **4.** Generating ideas about words

PET (Positron Emission Tomography) scans

show the brain in action. The bright colors in the four scans above indicate where your brain is active as you use language.

BRAIN QUIZ

What's wrong with this paragraph? Possibly it's just slightly unusual. You should try now and find out what's going through my mind as I pick out my words with caution. Don't look through it too quickly – study it analytically and in a painstaking way. With a bit of luck – and your thinking brain's vast capacity for brilliant thought – you should find what is so unfamiliar about it. Tax your mind if you don't crack it at first and try again. Don't miss anything. It isn't that difficult!   **Solution**

Practice makes perfect

These scans show the difference between a boy playing a computer game for the first time (left – lots of activity) and after two months of practice (right – very little activity).

Areas of the cerebral cortex (right)

1. Movement	**5.** Vision
2. Basic movement	**6.** Hearing
3. Sensation	**7.** Speech
4. Visual association	**8.** Behavior

Brain exercises

If you solved the puzzle above, you did it using the reasoning powers of your cerebral cortex (just 0.4 inch under the hair on your head!)

faCT: Iq STaNDS FoR iNTeLLiGeNCe QuoTieNT. ONe DeFiNiTioN oF iT iS BeiNG aBLe To THiNK LaTeRaLLY. liKe ReaLiZiNG WHaT'S GoiNG oN NoW. tHaT iS THaT THe uSuaL WaY oF uSiNG CaPiTaLS aND LoWeR-CaSe LeTTeRS HaS BeeN ReVeRSeD (eXCePT FoR VoWeLS).

By working your brain like this, you will improve it. Experiments have shown that learning to play with toys (and doing quizzes) actually thickens the cerebral cortex as the 10 billion nerve cells make more connections with one another. It's happening now! It works best in childhood, so the younger you are when you learn something, the better. Any adult who tries to take up the piano will tell you that!

The most common letter in the English language – e – is nowhere to be seen in the **BRAIN QUIZ** box. All the other letters of the alphabet are used.

The Cerebral Cortex

The two cerebral hemispheres cover the brain stem like a mushroom covers its stalk. The outer layer, called the cortex, looks wrinkled because of its many folds. This gray matter is like the bark that covers a tree. It is only about 0.078 inch thick. Its folds increase the total area by three times what it would be if it were smooth. The gray matter packed into your skull would roughly cover the surface of your pillow if you could iron it out!

Your **dominant cerebral hemisphere (1)** if you are right-handed is the left one. It mostly controls reading, writing, reasoning, and arithmetic. Your other hemisphere deals more with the emotional and creative areas of your life. A thick bundle of nerves called the **corpus callosum (2)** links the two hemispheres and enables them to share things like learning and memory, attention, and awareness. The dominant hemisphere keeps the whole show running smoothly. The **basal ganglia (3)** are large collections of nerve cell bodies that (with the cerebellum) keep body movements smooth and coordinated.

MAN TAN

In the spring of 1861, a man who for 21 years had been able to say only the word "tan" died. He understood words when spoken to and could communicate by using hand signals and facial expressions. After his death an area the size of a hen's egg was found to be missing from his left cerebral hemisphere. This was a scientific milestone, as it meant that language — at least part of it — could be traced to one particular area of the brain. Much of our information about the workings of the brain has come from the study of damaged brains like Tan's.

Temporal lobe

Frontal lobes

Protecting and Feeding the Brain

The most sensitive part of the brain:

the meninges

The bony plates that form your skull will protect your brain from everyday bumps, but the layers of the meninges that line the inside of the cranium provide a second and less obvious line of defense. The brain floats within this vital liquid cushion (see p. 18), which, although only amounting to about half a cupful (5 ounces) in total, is still an important shock absorber against blows to the head.

Right now your heart is pumping out about five quarts of blood every minute. And about 20% of this is sent to the head up the four main arteries. Your brain is taking more oxygen out of this blood at the moment than any other part of your body. It uses 20% of all the oxygen your lungs breathe in. The brain runs on this oxygen and on glucose (sugar). It needs nothing else. Every day this "computer," which is 85% water, uses no more than about the same amount of energy as a 10-watt light bulb.

FACE FACTS

Head wounds often look worse than they actually are. This is because the scalp has the richest supply of blood anywhere on the surface of your body and cuts bleed especially heavily.

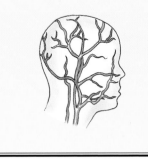

Meningitis

People get meningitis when germs get into the meninges. It's serious because these germs can easily spread from here to the brain. Some of the main symptoms are headache, fever, vomiting, lethargy, and a stiff neck. It needs urgent treatment. The diagnosis is usually made by passing a thin steel needle between the bones of the spine into the cerebrospinal fluid and finding the germ.

FIRST AID

Brain cells are not able to store energy like other body cells. This is why they die in minutes if their blood and oxygen supply is cut off. You can learn how to deal with this emergency in first-aid classes. The basis of the procedure called resuscitation is as easy as ABC.

A=Airway. Keep it open so air gets to the patient's lungs.
B=Breathing. If the patient isn't, you must help him or her breathe.
C=Circulation. If blood isn't moving around the body, you must give CPR – cardiopulmonary resuscitation.

Ever seen a rabbit in glasses?

Carrots contain carotene, which helps make vitamin A in your body. Vitamin A is necessary to see in the dark. This is the basis for the old wives' tale about carrots making you see better at night!

USE YOUR HEAD

Your scalp moves very easily over your skull. This is because the fibrous tissue in the layer just above the bone is very loosely attached. You can test this yourself by massaging your own scalp. It's interesting to think that the thoughts you are having about this matter are coming from only a few fractions of an inch below your massaging fingers.

The Meninges and Blood Vessels

The brain is covered by three layers of tissue called the meninges. The outer layer is tough and leathery. There is cerebrospinal fluid between the middle and inner meninges. Blood vessels run over the brain's cerebral cortex.

Dura mater
The tough outer layer of the meninges.

Pia mater
The delicate inner layer of the meninges.

The **arteries** (red) carry blood to the brain.

Arachnoid mater
The middle layer of the meninges resembles a spider web.

The **veins** (blue) carry blood away from the brain and back to the heart.

The **scalp** is made up of five layers of tissue. The tissue under the skin has some fat, but it is so firmly bound down with fibrous tissue that even the heaviest people do not get "fat" on the top of their heads! There just isn't enough space.

Head Lines

The most specialized lines of communication anywhere in the body: the cranial nerves

At the top of your body, as you may have noticed, is your Big Head. It's large in comparison to other animal heads because of its big brain. Humans need brains this size to cope with all the information coming in and out of an upright body, and to do all the things that can be done with two hands – free now to be used for skilled tasks rather than for walking on all fours. Right now, 12 pairs of cranial nerves are carrying information *to* your brain and commands *from* it. These nerves pass out of the base of your skull through holes called the foramina. The complex receptors at the ends of some of these nerves – at the eyes, the tongue, the nose, and the ears – are found nowhere else in the body!

Head movement

Head movement is a very important thing to have, especially for directing vison. Watching a tennis match is a simple example.

Your bony skull is carried on the first cervical vertebra (atlas), like the world on the shoulders of Atlas in Greek mythology. Smooth joints between the atlas bone and your skull allow you to nod your head as you say "Yes." Subtle movements are taking place at this joint right now while your eyes move and you read *down* the page.

As you look at the skull from the side, it seems to be perched rather precariously on the smaller bones of the vertebral column. However, powerful muscles – mainly at the back of your neck – keep it safe and steady on your shoulders. Under the atlas bone is the second cervical vertebra (axis). This bone has a peg at the front that sticks up and "locks" into the atlas bone above. This pivot joint enables you to shake your head and signal "No." You are moving it slightly (and your eyes, too) while you read *across* the page. These movements are performed by the muscles around the neck (see pp. 12-13).

Four eyes – no brain

The most poisonous creature in the sea is the box jellyfish (or sea wasp), found along the North Australian coast and around Southeast Asia. Each of its deadly body's four sides has an eye complete with lens and cornea. These eyes can certainly "see" because the jellyfish can move away from anything it finds threatening. But no one knows what they are connected to. Your cranial nerves can be traced as they run from organs like your eyes into your brain. But where in the transparent body of this eerie monster is the brain that receives the messages from those four eyes?

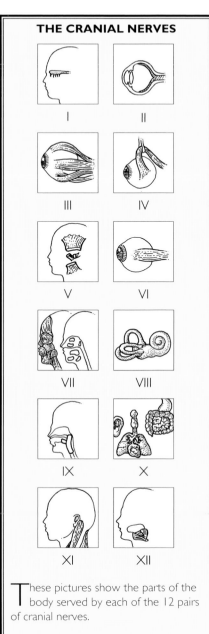

THE CRANIAL NERVES

I   II   III   IV   V   VI   VII   VIII   IX   X   XI   XII

These pictures show the parts of the body served by each of the 12 pairs of cranial nerves.

The Cranial Nerves

Traditionally the 12 pairs of cranial nerves are numbered using Roman numerals. The vagus (*vagus* means "wandering") nerve is the only one of the 12 to leave the head and neck.

I. The **olfactory nerve** of smell.

II. The **optic nerve** from the retina of the eye.

III. The **oculomotor nerve** controls four of the six muscles that move each eye.

IV. The **trochlear nerve** controls another muscle that moves the eye.

V. The **trigeminal nerve** carries messages of sensation from the face, nose, and mouth.

VI. The **abducens nerve** controls another muscle that moves the eye.

The arrows point to only one nerve in each pair.

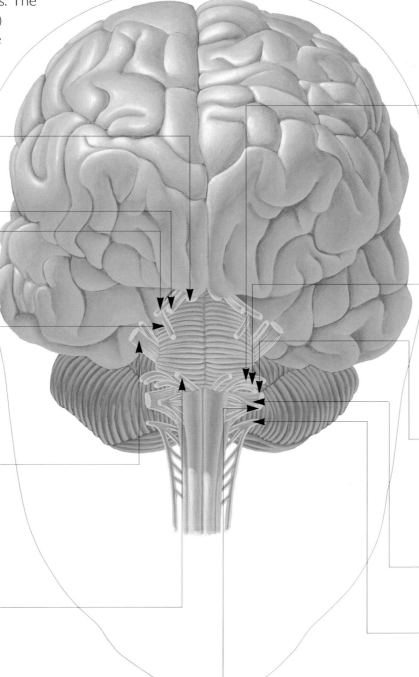

VII. The **facial nerve** controls the muscles of facial expression and the smallest muscle in the body – the stapedius – inside the ear. It also carries the sensation of taste from the front two thirds of the tongue as well as controlling four of the six salivary glands and the muscles of the pharynx.

VIII. The **vestibulocochlear nerve.** The vestibular part deals with balance, and the cochlear part with hearing.

IX. The **glossopharyngeal nerve** carries taste sensation from the back third of the tongue. It supplies the parotid salivary glands and some of the swallowing muscles as well as sensations from the back of the mouth and pharynx.

X. The **vagus nerve** "wanders" down the body to control the heartbeat, breathing muscles, gut mobility, and some of the liver and kidney functions.

XI. The **accessory nerve** controls some of the neck muscles.

XII. The **hypoglossal nerve** controls the muscles that move the tongue.

Vision

The head's greatest source of information:

the eye

Your eyes are obviously open as you read this, but one of the best ways to appreciate the most complex visual system of any animal is to close your eyes. Do it now for a few seconds . . .

Most of us have an uneasy, vulnerable, and slightly lonely feeling when deprived of sight. Even after a few seconds, there is great relief when we can open our eyes and rejoin the colorful visual world.

Down each optic nerve of your two eyes come thousands of millions of pieces of fresh information every second. Ten million shades of light and seven million of color are detected by a human's richest sense. Seventy-five percent of all the information that your brain will gather today will come from your eyes. Sometimes your eyes are likened to a TV camera – but there is a profound difference. Vision is in your brain – not in your eye. The information coming into your head is assembled into what you "see" by the part of the brain called the visual cortex (see opposite p. 31). It is here that electrical signals from the retina are given real meaning. Damage to the visual cortex can blind you even if your eyes are in perfectly good working order.

Eyes bigger than its stomach

The muscles that you use to roll your eyes are used by toads for a quite different job. Toads have no teeth in their lower jaw. This is unfortunate when you like to eat insects. So the toad lowers its eye muscles through a kind of trapdoor in its eye sockets and holds the insects with them while its upper teeth chew. The only disadvantage is that the toad can't see when it eats, but maybe you'd close your eyes too if someone put a plate of beetles down in front of you!

Tea for two

Different areas of your visual cortex handle different aspects of what you see. A lady named Gisela Leibold damaged the area where her eyes "saw" and processed movements of images. One big problem for her was that she couldn't pour a cup of tea without overfilling the cup. She couldn't see it filling up – just lots of "frozen" images of a teapot, a stream of tea from the spout, a cup with more and more tea in it, but no movement! She solved the problem by marking the inside of her cup near the top. When the line disappeared, she stopped pouring.

The Eye

Two eyes at the front of your head have adapted to provide you with a precise and focused view of the world around you. Less efficient than an owl's at night, not as keen as a hawk's in the day, not as wide-ranging as a deer's in the forest, your eyes can nevertheless move quickly from a book to a distant star, see colors, adapt to changes in light, estimate distances and direction, and bring two images into one for perfect 3-D vision.

The **retina** contains light-sensitive cells – the rods and cones.

Rods are the 125 million cells sensitive to the brightness of light.

Cones are the 7 million cells that detect color. There are three types and each is sensitive to either red, blue, or green.

The **lens** focuses light onto the retina.

The **pupil** is the hole through which light enters the eye. In the mirror yours looks like a dark spot in the center of each eye.

The **iris** is colored either blue, green, gray, or brown, and can make the pupil bigger or smaller depending on the amount of light.

The **sclera** is the tough coat that covers the eyeball. It is the "white" of the eye.

The **optic nerve** carries messages about light intensity and color to the brain.

The **cornea** is transparent and covers the front of the eye.

Hearing

The (middle) ear: the site where more is accomplished per square inch than anywhere else in your body

USE YOUR HEAD

Gently place the tips of your fingers just inside your ears. Now clench your fists. The rumbling noise is the sound of your muscles at work.

Listen to what you can hear at the moment. Maybe the TV is on or a bird is singing. Perhaps someone is talking. Whatever sound is being produced around you, some of its energy is traveling through the air to your ear. So, like the ripple from a stone thrown into a pond, these waves of sound are reaching you now.

As they do, the part of your ear that you can see in a mirror (the pinna) is collecting them and channeling them down the canal to your eardrum. It's vibrating now – slowly for low sounds and faster for the higher ones. These vibrations pass across the three smallest bones in your body. This is the "bridge of bones" to your inner ear. Here lies the greatest wonder of the ear. This is where you can pick out one voice at a noisy party or hear from a low hum right up to a high-pitched wailing shriek. Here the sound waves (vibrations) are turned into nerve impulses that travel to your brain up the eighth cranial nerve (see p. 35). When they reach your auditory cortex – well, you are listening to the result now.

Internal spirit level

The very first sense organ may have been a spirit level, a simple liquid-and-air balance organ, in a jellyfish. You can still see these if you look closely at the base of a tentacle (don't get stung). When a sudden wave sweeps across the creature and tilts this spirit level, the jellyfish can react and right itself because the surface of the liquid returns to a level horizontal line. Your inner ear has a similar balance mechanism. On the top of the cochlea are three semicircular tubes set at right angles to one another. They contain a liquid that moves when you move your head. Messages from these tubes enable your brain to readjust your position. So you may not be able to sting, but you do have something in common with the most poisonous creature in the sea (see p. 34).

'Ear, 'ear

The first airborne communications were probably between insects. Many insects have ears on places other than their heads. Butterflies have them at the base of their wings, mosquitoes on their antennae, and some grasshoppers below their knees! This may seem funny, but for these creatures hearing can be the difference between life and death. The praying mantis has a special ear where you have a belly button, just to listen for the hunting cry of the bat that likes to eat it!

Noises in the dark

A normal ear can tell the differences among about 40,000 different sounds. You have two ears, just as you have two eyes, so they can work together to locate the source of sound and find things in a 3-D world. Your ears are much better at locating sounds coming from the left or the right than from high up or low down. A barn owl has one ear higher than the other so it can locate the sound of a mouse scurrying below in the dark.

FACE FACTS

Humans have a tremendous range of hearing: from the noise of a jet engine to a mosquito buzzing. The power of a mosquito buzzing is so low that it would take (in watts) a hundred thousand billion buzzes to light a reading lamp!

The Ear

The ear can be divided into three parts: the outer ear (pinna and auditory canal); the middle ear (the cavity inside the skull bone that contains the hammer, anvil, and stapes); and the inner ear, which also deals with balance.

The three small bones in the middle ear are named after their shapes. They carry the sound from the **eardrum** to the **auditory nerve.**

Eardrum

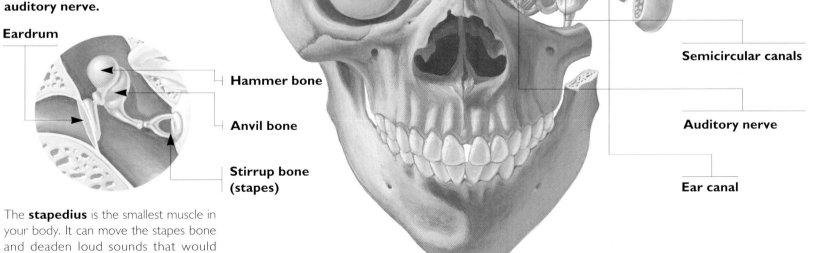

Hammer bone

Anvil bone

Stirrup bone (stapes)

Cochlea

Pinna

Eardrum

Semicircular canals

Auditory nerve

Ear canal

The **stapedius** is the smallest muscle in your body. It can move the stapes bone and deaden loud sounds that would otherwise damage your hearing.

Breathing, Smelling, and Eating

The nose: the only visible part of your respiratory system

One thing is certain, right now your head is inhaling and exhaling air. If you spent the whole of today resting, you would take about 12 breaths every minute, and each one of those breaths would take in about 13.5 fluid ounces of air. In a day this means you would breathe a total of about 1,850 gallons. Some of this air is now entering the upper part of the airways of your head (from your nose to your sinuses and your pharynx) and swirling around these cavities. It's being cleaned, warmed, and moistened before it travels in a few seconds from now down to your lungs. By the time it reaches the inside of your chest, it is as warm and damp as a tropical jungle.

Today the small glands lining the inside of your nose will produce an amazing one quart of fluid to trap and kill the dust, germs, and other debris that you will breathe in with the 1,850 gallons of air. You won't notice much of this as tiny brushes (cilia) gently waft and sweep all this fluid back down your throat, where it is eventually swallowed and destroyed by stomach acid.

Smelling

The olfactory (smelling) nerves enter the brain via the limbic system at a lower level than nerves for the other senses. Smell is the chief sense for many animals. Although smell is a primitive sense, it is also a very complicated one. The eye recognizes three primary colors and the tongue four basic tastes, but no one has ever managed to simplify smell in this way. One theory proposes seven primary smells: floral, musky, camphorous, peppermint, ethereal, pungent, and putrid.

FACE FACTS
The air is warmed in your nose by blood running in large veins just under the surface of the lining of the nasal cavity. Because of the size and large numbers of these veins and the position they are in, nosebleeds are quite common and may be quite heavy.

USE YOUR HEAD
Smell is the one sense that gets bored very easily. Put a small dab of a smelly substance like perfume on your upper lip just below your nose. For a short while you'll appreciate the smell, but quite quickly your brain will block it out and you'll soon stop noticing it. This can be very useful and is the reason why sewer workers can still enjoy their lunch while at work.

The hole through which nearly all of your body has traveled: your mouth

Over 99% of the body now reading this book has traveled through your mouth! Think back to the main meal you had yesterday. Since you ate it, it has been broken down (digestion) in your bowel, moved across the bowel wall (absorption), and now is becoming part of you (assimilation). Fate has cast food and your head together forever. Your head has your mouth on its face. This is where that meal, like all the food you'll ever eat, entered your body. That food set off your senses of smell and taste so that your head realized what was in store for it. Your head began digestion by chewing and chopping up the food. The food continued this process along by triggering the six salivary glands around your mouth. These added the first chemicals (enzymes) to break down the food. Then your head moved (swallowed) the food in mouthfuls down your esophagus and into your stomach.

The tongue
The tongue is the only muscle in your body that is loose at one end!

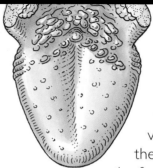

The Nose and Mouth

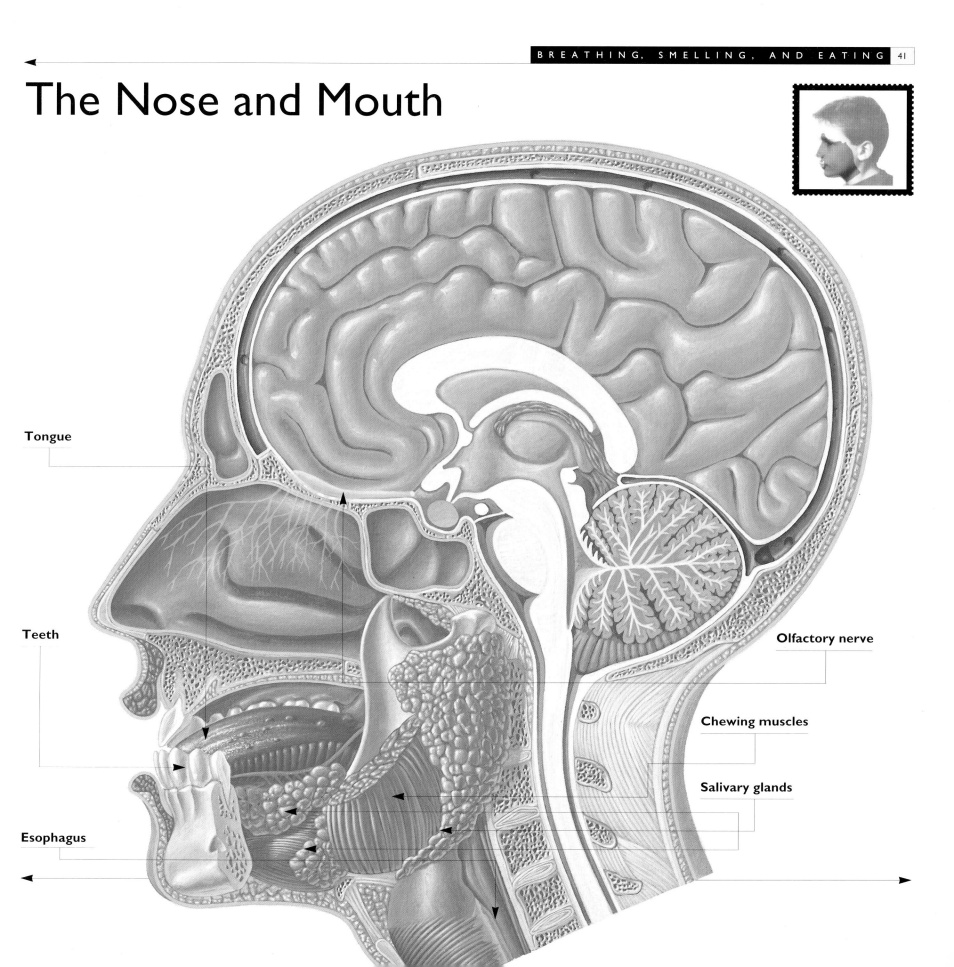

Tongue

Teeth

Esophagus

Olfactory nerve

Chewing muscles

Salivary glands

Making Faces

The most intricate signaling equipment in the world: the facial muscles

Touch your face. Messages about skin texture and body temperature flash to your brain, but what you can't tell from touch is the image you show to the rest of the world. How do you think your face looks now? While you are reading it's probably quite expressionless, but if a friend were to walk in, the hundred or so muscles under your skin would start their small, subtle contractions to signal your mood and your feelings about the other person. The signals to move these muscles of facial expression are coming from your brain's motor cortex and are easy to control. However, there is also a lot of subconscious input from the lower brain as the messages travel to your face, and these are not easy to control. This is what makes good acting very difficult.

FACE FACTS

How many faces do you think are stored in your brain's memory bank? How many people would you recognize if you saw them today? Not just family, friends at school, or aunts and uncles you see once a year, but all the sports and movie stars you've seen in films, on TV, and in magazines? There are probably thousands. And as you were reading that, I bet some of their images popped into your head without you realizing what was happening.

Faces are so important to humans that there is even one area of the brain set aside just for face recognition. This was discovered when people who had damaged this area found that they could see and name objects, but couldn't recognize the faces of even their close family.

Facial expressions

Faces all over the world show six basic emotions. These are anger, disgust, fear, happiness, sadness, and surprise. Even those blind from birth make these expressions. This supports the idea that these feelings are not learned but programmed into your brain's "hard disk" before you were born.

Happiness

Sadness

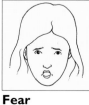

Anger

Surprise

Fear

Disgust

USE YOUR HEAD

What sort of smile do you have? From the moment when you first smiled at about six weeks old, your smiles have been giving away some of your innermost feelings. There are three basic types.

1. The Mona Lisa smile. This is the mysterious smoldering smile when the corners of the mouth are pulled up and out and the eyes wrinkle. It lasts 3-4 seconds and is almost impossible to fake.

2. The Snarl smile, when the main movement of the mouth is to raise the upper lip, is a rather false, forced smile with no use of the eyes.

3. The Toothpaste smile. The lips are pulled well back to expose the teeth. It is much loved by people who present TV programs and advertise toothpaste. Most smiles are a mixture of these three types. Look in the mirror and check yours.

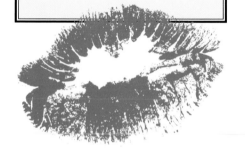

The Facial Muscles

These are the main muscles of facial expression. They signal feelings, open and shut the eyes and mouth, and move the lips and cheeks when you speak. Facial muscles are unusual since many are connected to skin or other muscles rather than bone. They tend to be arranged in a circular fashion around the orifices of the face.

The **frontalis** muscles raise the eyebrows in surprise.

The **corrugator supercilii** muscles (hidden by the frontalis) pull the eyebrows together to frown.

The **orbicularis oculi** muscles "screw" up the eyes in intense light (and are responsible for the crow's-feet of old age).

The **masseter** of the jaw is used for biting. The **buccinator** (hidden by the masseter) is the main muscle of the cheek, used for chewing and playing the trumpet!

The **zygomaticus major** muscles raise the corners of the mouth when you smile.

The **depressor labii inferioris** pulls the lower lip down to pout.

The **levator labii superioris** muscles open the lips and flare the nostrils.

The **depressor anguli oris** pulls the mouth down to grimace.

The **orbicularis oris** is the kissing muscle.

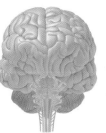